Beautiful Autumn
For Kids

Nature Books for Kids
By K. Bennett
Mendon Cottage Books

JD-Biz Publishing

Download Free Books!
http://MendonCottageBooks.com

Purchase at Amazon.com

Table of Contents

Introduction

Autumn is a second spring when every leaf is a flower

~ Albert Camus

Autumn: Autumn is an amazing season that comes between summer and winter. You will know it is autumn when the weather starts to get a little colder, the sunlight shines a little less and lots of plants stop making good food to eat.

Autumn is also a time of harvest for fruits and vegetables. Do you know what harvest means? This is when farmers pick the ripe fruits and vegetables that are ready to eat. Yum! Yum!

One of the biggest things you will see in autumn is lots of beautiful leaves on trees with bright colors like red, yellow, orange, and brown!

Do you know why trees stop being green and turn into different colors?
Keep reading to find out!

Why do the leaves change color?

Photosynthesis plays a very important part in the changing of the leaves. Do you remember what this big word means?

Leaves: The leaves of a tree are not only pretty but very important. They use energy to make food or sugar that the tree needs to "eat." This process is called photosynthesis.

In our book *"Beautiful Summer for Kids,"* we explained why sunlight is so important.

"Plants need the warm sun to grow…nice and strong. Sunlight is not only important for energy but also for food. After all, plants need to eat too!

To make their own food, plants need 3 things.

-Sunlight
-Water
-Carbon Dioxide

When plants get these three things they turn it into something called: GLUCOSE. And this is what the plants eat and store to get energy."

Leaves also have something called chlorophyll, which gives the leaves their bright green color. The more sunlight, the greener the leaves!

What happens during Autumn?

There is less sun shining during the months of autumn. Less sunlight means less green leaves. Less green leaves mean less chlorophyll. That is when other colors start to come out. Colors like red, yellow, orange, and brown!

Remember: Not all plants change their color during autumn. Do you remember what an Evergreen tree is? We talked about them in our book *"Beautiful Trees for Kids."*

There are two main types of trees. Those that lose their leaves during the changing seasons and those that keep their leaves green all year long.

-The ones that lose their leaves are called: **Deciduous.**

-The ones that stay green all the time are called: **Evergreen.**

Evergreen trees do lose leaves from time to time but it always makes new leaves before the old ones fall off! This is how it can stay green all the time.

Which one do you like best?

Autumn is also a very important season for animals in the wild. Can you guess what the animals are doing during these special months? Did you say… getting ready for winter? That's right!

Some animals, like squirrels, start to gather a lot more food just to have enough for the cold months. What a smart squirrel.

Other animals store food in their nests and dens. Some start to eat a lot of food so they can get very fat while other animals grow thick coats. This helps them to stay strong and warm when there is little food to eat and when it gets cold.

What about you? Do you do anything special during autumn?

Fun things to do!

Autumn is a great season to do lots of fun things. Here are seven ideas to think about. You might even like to try one of them.

1. Pick your own apples. If you don't live close to an apple orchard, ask your parents or a guardian to take you.

2. Go for a fun hay ride and take your friends with you!

3. Find the best and biggest pumpkin to make delicious pumpkin pie. Ask your parent or a guardian to help you get the ingredients and make it yourself.

4. Find a tree with the brightest autumn leaves, and see what different colors you can find. Can you see more red, brown, yellow, or orange? Which color variation do you like the best and why?

5. Go on a squirrel watch and see how they prepare for winter! Are they gathering lots of nuts or not? Take a notebook and write down anything interesting you see.

6. Visit a farm and help them to harvest their fruits and vegetables. Is it hard work or is it easy to do? There is only one way to find out!

7. Go for a nature walk and see if you can find any interesting creatures, trees, or flowers you have never seen before! Do they look different during autumn or the same?

If you don't like any of these ideas, there are many more fun activities online. Log on to the Familyshare.com website and search for *"15 fun things to do to celebrate fall."*

Have fun!

Source: http://familyshare.com/family/15-fun-things-to-do-to-celebrate-fall

Chapter 1: Harvest

What changes happen to planet Earth during autumn?

Autumn is a very important season for the earth, especially when it comes to food.

Lots of good food is harvested like: Brussels Sprouts, cabbage, beets, potatoes, squash, pumpkins, carrots, onions, leeks, pears, crapes, apples, and cranberries.

All of these fruits and vegetables are very good for us. Let's learn a little more about some of these autumn goodies!

Apples

Apple trees are very special trees with delicious fruit! Each year millions and millions of apples are sold around the world and many people enjoy them. What about you? What is your favorite apple? Red, green, yellow? And how do you like to eat them? Do you like them raw or cooked?

There are many different types of apples with cute names like: Pink Lady, Granny Smith, Fuji, Gala, Red delicious, Golden delicious, and many more.

Onions

Onions are made up of three main parts. The bulb, the leaves, and the roots, but the onion comes from the bulb at the base of the leaves.

Onions come in different shapes and colors, but they are usually smaller than a tennis ball. You can find then in different colors like white, red, yellow, and brown.

Onions are very good for your health but they can make you cry, when you cut them! Do you know why? It is because of the acid inside.

FUN FACTS FOR KIDS:

How are onions different from each other? Can you tell them apart? Here are some clues to help you!

Brown onions: These types of onions have a brown skin with a creamy inside. They have a strong flavor and lots of people love to cook with them.

White onions: They have a white skin and are white inside. They are good for cooking and very good for salads.

Red onions: They have red or purple looking skin. They can be eaten raw or cooked.

Yellow Onions: They look a lot like brown onions but they have a lighter skin that looks yellow with a creamy inside.

(Source: _www.Freshforkids.com.au_)

Squash

This vegetable is very healthy and good to eat. They are part of the pumpkin, cucumber, and melon family and come in lots of different sizes, colors, and shapes.

Squashes have interesting names like spaghetti, button, or scaloppini and vegetable marrow! They are also great for vitamin C, potassium, and fiber.

Squash is eaten in lots of different ways. You can boil it, microwave it, steam it, bake it, stir fry it, or deep fry it! The choice is up to you.

(Source: _www.Freshforkids.com.au_)

Pumpkins

This is probably one of the foods you know best. Do you like pumpkins? Great! If you don't, try it and see what it tastes like. You might be surprised at how good it is.

Pumpkins have a thick shell and are very tasty inside. They are not only orange but can be different colors like: red, green, white, and yellow. They give you lots of energy and are very good for you. Every year over one billion pounds of pumpkin is produced in the United States. That's a lot of pumpkin!

Pumpkin is very easy to cook. You can boil it, steam it, bake it, and even roast it.

(Source: *www.Sciencekids.co.nz*)

Carrots

Carrots are sometimes called the "king of the vegetables." This means they are very, very good for you! Many people around the world eat carrots every day and even Bugs Bunny likes them too!

Carrots are used in lots of different ways. You can find them in soups, salads, pastas, and even cakes. Carrots have very interesting names like: Nantes, Kurodo, Imperitor, and Dutch.

Carrots are full of fiber and beta carotene. Our body uses this important nutrient and changes it into Vitamin A, and this helps us to have great night vision. Have you ever heard that if you eat lots of carrots you will be able to see in the dark? Try it and see if it works!

These are just some of the amazing fruits and vegetables harvested during the autumn months. There are many more to add. Can you think of anything else?

Make a list and share your findings with others. **Remember:** Sharing is caring!

Happy harvesting explorers!

(Source: *www.Freshforkids.com.au*)

Chapter 2: Migration

Food is not the only thing that changes during autumn. Lots of things happen in the animal kingdom too! This is the time of great migrations. Do you know what migration means, and why animals move around from one place to another?

Migration:

This word basically means when animals move from one place to another and then back again. Think of it like a ticket from Miami to New York and then back to Miami again!

These animals use many different ways to find their way. Some use the sun, others use the stars, and many use the earth's magnetic field.

Of course, some animals do not make the trip back home. For example, salmon travel to breeding grounds to have their young and die there. But many animals return to their home, and during autumn some very special creatures make a long journey to other places to escape the cold.

Creatures like: snow geese, monarch butterflies, swallows, Rufous hummingbirds, rattle snakes, gopher snakes, humpback whales, dolphins, wild caribou, and many more!

Let's talk a little bit about two of the most amazing migrations ever seen on planet earth.

Monarch Butterflies:

These cute little butterflies can fly for two to three thousand miles from the United States to Mexico. Can you guess why? Yes! It is much too cold for them to stay during winter, so they make the long journey to warmer places.

These little butterflies are very smart and they know exactly when to leave and then to come back. You might be thinking they don't live long enough to make the trip back and forth and you would be right!

Usually, about five generations of butterflies complete the migration journey from the United States to Mexico and back again.

Here's a question for you: How do they know **when** to leave and **when** to go back?

Humpback Whales:

These beautiful whales travel for over three thousand miles to warmer waters. Some even travel as much as five thousand miles or even more. That is a very long journey!

The whales travel all the way to the Great Barrier Reef in Australia to have their babies. Other species travel to other places like South Africa, New Zealand, and South America.

One of the most important reasons for this migration is because of food. In warmer waters, whales can find lots of food to eat and this can keep them alive until the winter season is over.

Isn't nature amazing?

FUN FACTS FOR KIDS:

There are twelve months in a calendar year. Can you guess which months are: Spring, Summer, Autumn, and Winter?

Spring: March, April, and May

Summer: June, July, and August

Autumn: September, October and November (This season is also called: Fall)

Winter: December, January, and February.

Which season do you like best? Think about your reasons, write them down or share with others!

Fun autumn activity!

There are lots of fun things you might like to try during this season. Have you ever played *Find the Pumpkin* before?

This great game comes from *Kidsactivities.net* and the writer Barbara Shelby. Are you ready?

FIND THE PUMPKIN!

These are the supplies you will need:

-Ten pieces of white paper – You might choose another color if you don't like white.

- Five pieces of yellow paper - Mix and match colors if you don't want this one. Just try to use autumn colors!

- Five pieces of orange paper – You might choose red or brown too!
- A crayon – Choose a fun color

- Scissors (Get an adult to help you and be careful)

These directions come from the website:

1. Draw ten white pumpkins, five yellow pumpkins, and five orange pumpkins. (Or adjust the numbers to reflect the number of your group) – **Change the colors around if you don't like these choices!**

2. Cut out all the pumpkins.

3. Decorate each pumpkin with a funny face.

4. Write the number 1 on the backs of the white pumpkins.

5. Write the number 5 on the backs of the yellow pumpkins.

6. Write the number 10 on the backs of the orange pumpkins.

7. Have an adult hide all of the pumpkins.

8. Now try to find as many pumpkins as you can before they all have been found.

9. Players will add up the numbers of collected pumpkins. The player with the most points wins! This can also be played in teams.

(Credit: http://www.kidactivities.net/category/Seasonal-FallAutumn-Games.aspx)

If you don't like this game, make a variation of it or search for more online.

Have a great time!

Chapter 3: Facts about Autumn

I hope you enjoyed this book on Beautiful Autumn! Here are just a few more neat facts you may like to learn about.

- Bobbing for apples is something people love to do in autumn. Did you know this tradition started in Rome? There are lots of apple bobbing competitions around the world, but a man named Ashrita Furman is the New York apple bobbing champion. He bobbed 34 apples in just one minute!

- A man named Joel Jarvis grew the largest squash ever. Guess how much it weighed? 1,486.6 pounds! That is a very heavy squash! When they asked him how his squash got so big, he said "time, effort, and lots of tender-loving care." What about you? Do you think you could grow something that big?

- Pumpkins are grown all over the world. There is only one continent in the world where pumpkins are not grown…can you guess which one? Here are the seven continents to help you remember.

-Africa

-Antarctica

-Australia / Oceania

-Asia

-Europe

-North America

-South America

Which continent did you pick? Did you choose number 2? Great job! Yes, **Antarctica** is the only place in the world where pumpkins are not grown! It is far too cold for them to grow there.

- If you eat too many carrots you can turn orange! Wow…what do you think about that?

- The Greeks had a cute name for carrots. They called them *Philtrons*, which means love charm. The Greeks felt that people got more loving if they ate carrots. Isn't that cute?

- The Chinese give thanks for their summer harvest during autumn. It is called the Moon Festival.

(Source: *www.Todaysparent.com*)

KEEP LEARNING!

Autumn is one of the four seasons. And the reason why we have seasons is because of the earth's tilt towards the sun. Do you remember how many degrees it is tilted? Can you guess?

1- **14.76°** (Fourteen point seventy-six degrees)

2- **20.22°** (Twenty point twenty-two degrees)

3- **23.45°** (Twenty-three point forty-five degrees)

If you chose number 3 you are correct! This is what gives the earth the beautiful seasons during the year.

Vocabulary:

During the autumn season you will hear many different words that people use. Words like:

-Acorn

-Apple Cider

-Thanksgiving

-Chestnuts

-Cornucopia

-Crisp

-Harvest moon

-Persimmon

-Boating

-Reap

-Maize

-Sleet

-Journey

-Migration

-Gourd

-Hayride

-Deciduous

-Feast

-Quilt

-Cobweb

-Haystack

-Chilly

-Rake

-Autumnal Equinox

-Pine Cone

Do you know what any of these words mean? If you are not sure, ask your parent or a guardian's permission to search for the definition. I hope you learn something new! (*www.dictionary.com*)

Conclusion:

In conclusion: Autumn is a very special and does amazing things for our planet. Here are a few more ideas to help you learn more about this wonderful season!

Why don't you research how animals adapt or change during this season? To help you get started…here are a few animals that do interesting things during autumn.

- **The Ptarmigan** This amazing bird gets pretty white feathers during autumn! This helps them to hide from their enemies and also helps them to get ready for winter. The feathers grow so long it covers their feet, legs and toes!

- **Arctic Foxes** These animals love to change their clothes into a pretty white fur coat in autumn. This coat is nice and long and covers their feet too. (This helps them to hide from their enemies and walk better when the snow starts to fall.)

- **Molting** This is when animals change their coats for much thicker and lighter colored coats to get ready for winter.

- **Diet** Some birds eat caterpillars and other insects during spring and summer, but when autumn comes they start to eat seeds. Why? If you do not know the answer, do some research and see what you find. Don't forget to share your findings with others and get permission before you search online.

Something else to think about...

Think of show and tell at school or another school project. Can you talk about autumn activities and share with your teacher and classmates? Maybe you can tell them why you like it so much and what makes it different from other seasons!

What about making glow in the dark pumpkins, leaf people, or leaf rubbings are another great idea!

A nature walk is another great choice. On your walk, why don't you look at the color of the leaves and see how different they are from other trees?

If you live in a place where the trees do not change color, can you find some other way to tell the change in the season? For example, are there butterflies flying around? What about birds? Do you hear new sounds you haven't heard before or see new things you haven't seen before?

Just one more!

Fall starts on the Autumn Equinox. Do you know what this means? Become a science journalist and start digging!

You might decide to use this subject as a science project and explain how the planet earth changes during the months of September, October, and November in the Northern Hemisphere.

And in the Southern Hemisphere, it would be March, April and May! How is this possible, and how different is one place from the other?

You may choose to make this subject a science project or an experiment. If you do, don't forget the steps you need to do to make it a good science project.

Steps:

1 – You need to ask a **question** that can be answered by observation or experimentation. Make it a very interesting question so your classmates and teachers will be excited to learn the answer!

2 – The next step is to state a **Hypothesis**. This is a big word, it basically means an educated guess about what you think will be the outcome of your experiment.

So your hypothesis is what you think the results of your project will be when your research is all done!

3 – Next thing to think about is: **Procedure.** This is very important. Procedure will help you to find the answer to your question and prove what you are trying to say. It is a step by step plan of how the experiment is going to go.

4 – **Results**. You will need to show your results and all of the information you collected for your project.

5 – **Conclusion**. Finish up with what you learned and then answer the question you had in Step 1. If you are unable to answer the question, this is also a great place to put the reasons why the question cannot be answered.

(Source: *www.randroades.wcpss.net*)

I know you will have fun learning about beautiful autumn! And there are lots more you can still learn, if you just take the time to try. If you don't like the ideas in this book, put on your thinking cap and come up with your own conclusions!

I am sure you will do an amazing job! We hope you have enjoyed this book on Beautiful Autumn and always remember…

"Educating the mind without educating the heart is no education at all." - Aristotle

Happy Learning!

Author Bio

K. Bennett loves to write for both children and adults. Many different subjects are interesting to research, but writing for children is special to her heart.

Her favorite pastimes include reading, traveling and discovering new things. Each of these activities helps to fuel her imagination and acts like a blank canvas waiting for more stories.

She is intrigued with fantasy elements like hidden worlds and faraway lands. And basically anything that gets her imagination soaring to new heights!

Her writing credits include children books online, short stories for online magazines, and novellas listed at Amazon.com

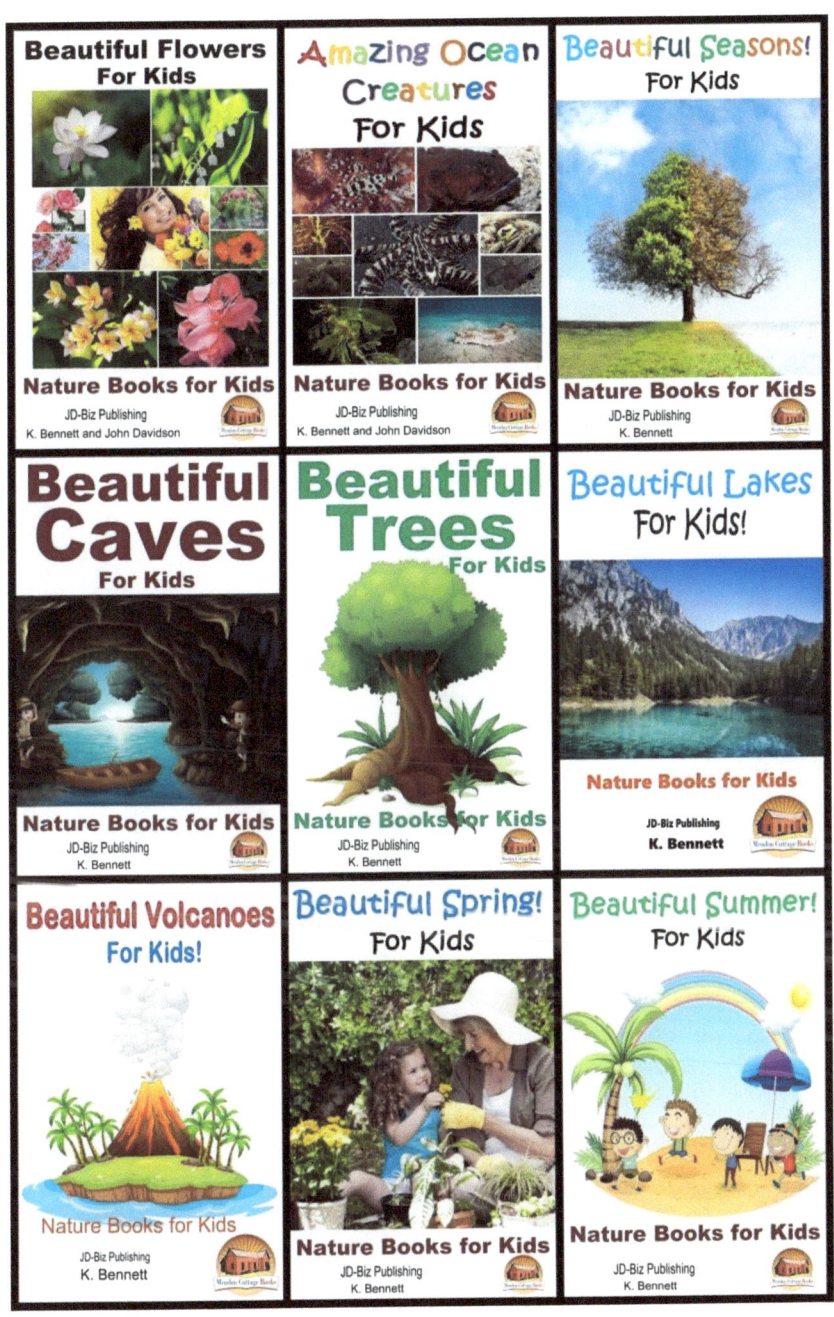

Our books are available at

1. Amazon.com

2. Barnes and Noble

3. Itunes

4. Kobo

5. Smashwords

6. Google Play Books

Download Free Books!
http://MendonCottageBooks.com

Publisher

JD-Biz Corp

P O Box 374

Mendon, Utah 84325

http://www.jd-biz.com/

www.ingramcontent.com/pod-product-compliance
Lightning Source LLC
Chambersburg PA
CBHW050850290526
45792CB00002B/594